Nestlé

# smarties®
# Chuckle factory

# Nestlé® smarties®

# Chuckle factory

Illustrated by Mike Phillips

Robinson Children's Books

First published in the UK by Robinson Children's Books,
an imprint of Constable + Robinson Ltd, 2000

Robinson + Constable Ltd
3 The Lanchesters
162 Fulham Palace Road
London
W6 9ER

Illustrations © Mike Phillips 2000

A copy of the British Library Cataloguing in Publication Data
for this title is available from the British Library

ISBN 1-84119-156-6

Printed and bound in Denmark

10 9 8 7 6 5 4 3 2 1

# Contents

# Introduction

Put in your order for any type of joke, any shape, any size, any colour, any make at all, a joke about a dog, a joke about an elephant or a joke about a polar bear - The Chuckle Factory can make it for you.

Today the factory is churning out the funniest and most ridiculous jokes about animals, but if you want to insult someone then the reject room is the place for you. There's some real crackers here. Carefully locked away behind the heavy iron gates are some totally monstrous jokes and ready for collection in the cold storage room are piles of real "cool" jokes. And finally, of course, there's the most important part of the factory - The Sweetie Factory - the part that makes all the chocolate jokes, the ice cream jokes and the jokes about the things we love to eat. But watch out for the ghosts, they do say the factory is haunted . . .

# Chapter One

How can you prevent an elephant from charging?
Take away his credit card.

Why are black cats such good singers?
They're very mewsical.

When it is unlucky to see a black cat?
When you're a mouse.

What do you call it when a witch's cat falls off her broomstick?
A catastrophe.

What do you get if you cross an owl with a witch?
A bird that's ugly but doesn't give a hoot.

What do you get if you cross a witch's cat with Father Christmas?
Santa Claws.


How do you get milk from a cat?
Steal her saucer.


What do you get if you cross a witch's cat with a canary?
A peeping tom.

What do you call a cat with eight legs that likes to swim?
An octopuss.

What has four legs, a tail, whiskers and flies?
A dead witch's cat.

What has four legs, a tail, whiskers and goes round and round for hours?
A black cat in a tumble-drier.

What's a vampire's favourite animal?
A giraffe.

What is Smokey the Elephant's middle name?
The.

What game do elephants play when they are in a car?
Squash.

One goldfish to his tankmate: "If there's no God, who changes the water?"

What do you get if you cross a werewolf with a hyena?
I don't know but if it laughs I'll join in.

"It's cruel," said the papa bear to his family on seeing a carload of humans, "to keep them caged up like that."

"Mummy," said the little lamb. "Can I go to an all-ram's school when I'm five."
"Don't be silly darling," said his mother who was a very aristocratic sheep. "That would be frightfully non-U."

What do you get if you cross a man-eating monster with a skunk?
A very ugly smell.

What do you get if you pour hot water down a rabbit hole?
Hot cross bunnies!

Jim: Our dog is just like one of the family.
Fred: Which one?

There was once a *puppy* called May who loved to pick quarrels with animals who were bigger than she was. One day she argued with a lion. The next day was the first of June.
Why?
Because that was the end of May!

What did the beaver say to the tree?
"It sure is good to gnaw you."

What do you get it you cross a hedgehog with a
giraffe?
A long-necked toothbrush.

Alex's class went on a nature study ramble.
"What do you call a thing with ten legs, red spots and
great big jaws, Sir?" asked Alex.
"I've no idea, why do you ask?" replied the teacher.
"Because one just crawled up your trouser leg."

Just before the Ark set sail, Noah saw his two sons fishing over the side. "Go easy on the bait, lads," he said. "Remember I've only got two worms."

Mary's class was taken to the Natural History Museum in London. "Did you enjoy yourself?" asked her mother when she got home.
"Oh yes," replied Mary. "But it was funny going to a dead zoo."

What do you get if you cross a yeti with a kangaroo? A fur coat with big pockets.

"What's the difference between a kangaroo, a lumberjack and a bag of peanuts?"
"A kangaroo hops and chews and a lumberjack chops and hews."
"Yes, but what's the bag of peanuts for?"
"For monkeys like you."

What do you get if you cross a sheepdog and a bunch of daisies?
Collie-flowers!

What do you get if you cross a zebra and a donkey?
A zeedonk.

What fish do dogs chase?
Catfish.

What do you get if you cross a skunk and an owl?
A bird that smells but doesn't give a hoot!

What do you get if you cross a cow and a camel?
Lumpy milkshakes!

What do you get if you cross an elephant and peanut butter?
Either peanut butter that never forgets, or an elephant that sticks to the roof of your mouth.

What do you get if you cross a kangaroo and a mink?
A fur jumper with pockets.

What dog smells of onions?
A hot dog.

What do you get if you cross a sheep and a
rainstorm?
A wet blanket.

Three animals were having a drink in a café, when the
owner asked for the money.
"I'm not paying," said the duck.
"I've only got one bill and I'm not breaking it."
"I've spent my last buck," said the deer.
"Then the duck'll have to pay," said the skunk.
"Getting here cost me my last scent."

A blind man was waiting to cross the road when a dog stopped and cocked its leg against him. The blind man felt in his pocket for a sweet, bent down, and offered it to the dog. A passer-by remarked what a very kind act that was considering what the dog had done. "Not at all," said the blind man. "I only wanted to find out which end to kick."

"My dog plays chess."
"Your dog plays chess? He must be really clever!"
"Oh, I don't know. I usually beat him three times out of four."

Would you like a duck egg for tea?
Only if you "quack" it for me.

What do you get if you cross a nun and a chicken?
A pecking order.

A man with a newt on his shoulder walked into a pub.
"What do you call him," asked the barmaid.
"Tiny," said the man.
"Why do you call him Tiny?"
"Because he's my newt!"

Who is the biggest gangster in the sea?
Al Caprawn.

What comes after cheese?
A mouse.

14

"Bring me a crocodile sandwich immediately."
"I'll make it snappy, sir."

Why did the woman take a load of hay to bed?
To feed her nightmare.

Why was the young kangaroo thrown out by his
mother?
For smoking in bed.

What's black and white and noisy?
A zebra with a drum kit.

A huge lion was roaring through the jungle when he
suddenly saw a tiny mouse. He stopped and snarled
at it menacingly. "You're very small," he growled
fiercely.
"Well, I've been ill," replied the mouse piteously.

This loaf is nice and warm!
It should be - the cat's been sitting on it all day!

Rabbits can multipy - but only a snake can be an adder.

If 20 dogs run after one dog, what time is it?
Twenty after one.

"My budgie lays square eggs."
"That's amazing! Can it talk as well?"
"Yes, but only one word."
"What's that?"
"Ouch!"

What do you get if you cross a cow with a mule?
Milk with a kick in it.

What lies at the bottom of the sea and shivers?
A nervous wreck.

What is cowhide most used for?
Holding cows together.

Why do bears wear fur coats?
They'd look silly in plastic macs.

How does an elephant go up a tree?
It stands on an acorn and waits for it to grow.

"Would you like to play with our new dog?"
"He looks very fierce. Does he bite?"
"That's what I want to find out."
"What's your new dog's name?"
"Dunno - he won't tell me."

First cat: How did you get on in the milk-drinking contest?
Second cat: Oh, I won by six laps!

**FOR SALE**

PEDIGREE BULLDOG
HOUSE TRAINED
EATS ANYTHING
VERY FOND OF CHILDREN

"Have you ever seen a man-eating tiger?"
"No, but in the café next door I once saw a man eating chicken!"

A large sailing ship was at anchor off the coast of Mauritius, and two dodos watched the sailors rowing ashore.
"We'd better hide," said the first dodo.
"Why?" asked the second.
"Because," said the first, "we're supposed to be extinct, silly!"

What's a cow's favourite love song?
When I Fall In Love, It Will Be For Heifer.

If a dog is tied to a rope 15 feet long, how can it reach a bone 30 feet away?
The rope isn't tied to anything!

There were ten zebras in the zoo. All but nine escaped. How many were left?
Nine!

What do you get if you cross a chicken with a cow?
Roost beef.

First lion: Every time I eat, I feel sick.
Second lion: I know. It's hard to keep a good man down.

Why did the pig run away from the pigsty?
He felt that the other pigs were taking him for grunted.

What do you call a multi-storey pig-pen?
A styscraper.

What do you get if you cross a crocodile with a flower?
I don't know, but I'm not going to smell it.

"Gosh, it's raining cats and dogs," said Suzie looking out of the kitchen window.
"I know," said her mother who had just come in.
"I've just stepped in a poodle!"

Why couldn't the butterfly go to the dance?
Because it was a moth-ball.

Why do elephants have flat feet?
From jumping out of tall trees.

Is it true that carrots are good for the eyesight?
Well you never see rabbits wearing glasses.

How can you tell if an elephant has been sleeping in
your bed?
The sheets are wrinkled and the bed smells of
peanuts.

Is the squirt from an elephant's trunk very
powerful?
Of course - a jumbo jet can keep 500 people in the
air for hours at a time.

What do you get if you cross a chicken with an
octopus?
A Sunday dinner where everybody gets a leg.

"Why are you crying, little boy?"
"'Cos we've just had to have our dog put down!" sobbed the lad.
"Was he mad?" asked the old lady.
"Well he wasn't too happy about it."

What's the difference between a wild camel and a bully?
One's a big, smelly, bad-tempered beast and the other is an animal.

Charlie: I'd like to talk to you in kangaroo-speak.
Clare: What would you say?
Charlie: Hop it!

# Chapter Two

What did the mummy snake say to the crying baby snake?
"Stop crying and viper your nose."

Why did the viper, viper nose?
Because the adder adder handkerchief.

How do you know when there's a monster under your bed?
Your nose touches the ceiling.

There was a big monster from Leek
Who, instead of a nose, had a beak.
It grew quite absurd
Till he looked like a bird.
He migrates at the end of the next week.

Why did the monster have green ears and a red nose?
So that he could hide in rhubarb patches.

What happened to the witch with an upside-down nose?
Every time she sneezed her hat blew off.

Wizard: You've got a Roman nose.
Witch: Like Julius Caesar?
Wizard: No, it's roamin' all over your face.

What usually runs in witches' families?
Noses.

One day a teacher came into her classroom and found a very rude word chalked on her blackboard. "I'm not going to scold," she said. "We're going to take care of this by the honour system. We'll all close our eyes and I'll count up to 100. When we open our eyes whoever wrote that will have tiptoed up to the board and erased it."

Everyone closed their eyes. "One, two, three," pitter pitter, "48, 49, 50," squeak, squeak "99, 100." Everyone opened their eyes and there, on the board, was another, even filthier word and above it was chalked, "The phantom writer strikes again."

Knock, knock.
Who's there?
Tristan Tristan who?
Tristan insect to really
get up your nose.

Witch: Doctor, I've got a head like a turnip, three ears, two noses and a mouth the wrong way round. What am I?
Doctor: Ugly.

Werewolf: Doctor, doctor, thank you so much for curing me.
Doctor: So you don't think you're a werewolf any more?
Werewolf: Absolutely not, I'm quite clear now - see my nose is nice and cold.

What do you call a vampire who gets up your nose?
Vic.

What has two heads, three hands, two noses and five feet?
A monster with spare parts.

Why did the teacher have her hair in a bun?
Because she had her nose in a hamburger.

Why did the monster take his nose apart?
To see what made it run.

Monster: Doctor, doctor, how do I stop my nose from running?
Doctor: Stick out your foot and trip it up.

Did you hear about the snake with a bad cold?
No! Tell me about the snake with a bad cold.
It had to viper nose.

Why did the witch put her broom in the washing machine?
She wanted a clean sweep.

What happened when the werewolf fell in the washing machine?
He became a wash-and-werewolf.

What does a black mamba do in the toilet?
Tries to wash his hands.

Girl: Mum, mum a monster's just bitten my foot off.
Mum: Well keep out of the kitchen, I've just washed the floor.

Teacher: What's the difference between a buffalo and a bison?
Student: You can't wash your hands in a buffalo, Miss.

# Chapter Three

Why did the cat put the letter M into the fridge?
Because it turns ice into mice.

Why is a polar bear cheap to have as a pet?
It lives on ice.

What was the fly doing on the ice cream?
Learning to ski.

What kind of money do yetis use?
Iced lolly.

What do you get if you cross a witch with an iceberg?
A cold spell.

How do ghosts like their drinks?
Ice ghoul.


Two witches lost their brooms and crash-landed on an iceberg.
"Do you think we'll be here long?" asked the first.
"No," said the second, "here comes the Titanic."


What does a yeti eat for dinner?
Ice-burgers.

What happened when the ice monster had a furious row with the zombie?
He gave him the cold shoulder.

Simon: My girlfriend and I fell out last night. She wanted to go and watch ice-skating, but I wanted to go to the football match.
Peter: What was the ice-skating like?

What happened when the ice monster ate a curry?
He blew his cool.

What did the Eskimo schoolboy say to the Eskimo schoolgirl?
"What's an ice girl like you doing in a place like this?"

On their first evening in their new home the bride went in to the kitchen to fix the drinks.
Five minutes she came back into the living room in tears.
"What's the matter, my angel?" asked her husband anxiously.
"Oh Derek!" she sobbed, "I put the ice cubes in hot water to wash them and they've disappeared!"

What's a polar bear's favourite food?
Iceburgers.

How do you know if an elephant's been in your fridge?
There are footprints in the butter.

Wally: If frozen water is iced water, what is frozen ink?
Sally: Iced ink.

Why did Darren put his father in the freezer?
He wanted ice-cold pop.

Why did the stupid witch keep her clothes in the fridge?
She liked to have something cool to slip into in the evening.

A woman went to the fridge to get some milk and all
she found was a disembodied hand there.
It was all fingers and thumbs.

Why did Ken keep his trumpet in the fridge?
Because he liked cool music.

Cannibal Boy: I've brought a friend home for dinner.
Cannibal Mum: Put him in the fridge and we'll have
him tomorrow.

What stays hot in the fridge?
A hamburger with too much mustard on it.

What did the mayonnaise say to the fridge?
Shut the door, I'm dressing.

What do you call the famous Italian artist who did his paintings sitting on the fridge?
Bottichilli.

When Angela had to write down on her exam paper the name of a liquid that won't freeze, she wrote "hot water".

What is brown one minute and white the next?
A rat in a deep-freeze.

What's another way to describe a duck?
A chicken with snowshoes.

What did the Eskimo children sing when one of their class was leaving school?
Freeze a jolly good fellow.

Spooky happenings at the supermarket! A customer was just leaning over the freezer looking for some frozen chips when ten fish fingers crept up and pulled him in . . .

Why did the monster drink 10 litres of anti-freeze?
So that he didn't have to buy a winter coat.

What kind of medicine does Dracula take for a cold?
Coffin medicine.

Why did the snowman call his dog Frost?
Because frost bites.

Teacher: Who knows what we mean by the Cold War?
Larry: Err, a snowball fight?

What did one Abominable Snowman say to the other?
"I'm afraid I just don't believe in people."

What do you get if you cross King Kong with a snowman?
Frostbite.

What exams do yetis take?
Snow levels.

What do you give a pony with a cold?
Cough Stirrup.

What is the Abominable Snowman's favourite book?
War and Frozen Peas.

How do Abominable Snowmen feel when they melt?
Abominable!

What do Abominable Snowmen call their offspring?
Chill-dren.

What did the Abominable Snowman do after he had
had his teeth pulled out?
He ate the dentist.

Where do Abominable Snowmen go to dance?
To snowballs.

Why did the skeleton stay out in the snow all night?
He was a numbskull.

What did the monster say when he saw Snow White
and the Seven Dwarfs?
"Yum, yum!"

There was a young yeti from Gloucester
Whose granny and grandfather lost 'er.
Next day she was found
In the snow-covered ground
But they didn't know how to defrost her.

Doctor, doctor, I keep thinking I'm the Abominable
Snowman.
Keep cool.

I
MET AN
ABOMINABLE
SNOWMAN

BY
ANNE TARTIC

Did you hear about the woman who was so keen on road safety that she always wore white at night? Last winter she was knocked down by a snowplough.

Why was the snowman no good at playing in the big match?
He got cold feet.

Ted and Fred were enjoying themselves in the snow.
"You can borrow my sledge if you like," said Ted.
"Thanks," said Fred. "We'll share it, shall we?"
"Yes," said Ted. "I'll have it going downhill and you can have it going uphill."

How do you know if your cat's got a bad cold?
He has cat-arrh.

Two shark fishermen were sitting on the side of their boat just off the coast of Florida, cooling their feet in the sea. Suddenly an enormous shark swam up and bit off one fisherman's leg.

"A shark's just bitten off my leg," yelled the fisherman.

"Which one?"

"I don't know. All sharks look the same to me."


Billy: I never had a sledge when I was a kid. We were too poor.

Milly, feeling sorry for him: What a shame! What did you do when it snowed?

Billy: Slid down the hills on my cousin.

Kevin: I'm really cool, you know.
Kieran: I always thought you were a cold fish.

Why is a football stadium cool?
It's full of fans.

What's hairy and damp and sits shivering at fairs?
A coconut with a cold.

Did you hear about the mad scientist who put
dynamite in his fridge?
They say he blew his cool

What does an octopus wear when it's cold?
A coat of arms.

What can a schoolboy keep and give away at the same time?
A cold.

What's a cold, evil candle called?
The wicked wick of the north.

Can the Abominable Snowman jump very high?
Hardly - he can only just clear his throat!

What goes "hum-choo, hum-choo"?
A bee with a cold.

What happened to the zombie who had a bad cold?
He said, "I'm dead-up wid fuddy jokes aboud zondies."

Doctor, doctor, what would you take for this cold?
Make me an offer.

Why do skeletons hate winter?
Because the cold goes right through them.

What's the difference between a bus driver and a cold in the head?
A bus driver knows the stops, and a cold in the head stops the nose.

And what goes into the water pink and comes out blue?
A swimmer on a cold day!

George knocked on the door of his friend's house. When his friend's mother answered he said, "Can Albert come out to play?"
"No," said the mother, "it's too cold."
"Well, then," said George, "can his football come out to play?"

Doctor, doctor, how can I stop my cold going to my chest?
Tie a knot in your neck.

Why can you run faster when you've got a cold?
Because you have a racing pulse and a running nose.

Teacher: Matthew, what is the climate of New Zealand?
Matthew: Very cold, Sir.
Teacher: Wrong.
Matthew: But Sir! When they send us meat, it always arrives frozen!

What is hairy and coughs?
A coconut with a cold.

Geography Teacher: What is the coldest place in the world?
Ann: Chile.

Lady (to a tramp who's asked for a meal): Do you like cold prunes and custard?
Tramp: I love it lady.
Lady: Well, call back later, it is very hot right now.

Young Horace was being taught how to box, but so far hadn't landed a single blow on his opponent.
"Don't worry, lad," said his teacher, "keep swinging, the draught might give him a cold."

It was raining, and the goalie had let several goals through. As he came off the pitch he sniffed, and said, "I think I've caught a cold."
"I'm pleased to hear you can catch something," replied a fellow player.

# Chapter Four

What do you get if you cross a skeleton with a
famous detective?
Sherlock bones.

What trees do ghouls like best?
Ceme-trees.

What did the baby ghost eat for dinner?
A boo-loney sandwich.

Why are graveyards so noisy?
Because of all the coffin.

How can you tell if a corpse is angry?
It flips it's lid.

How do undertakers speak?
Gravely.

When can't you bury people who live opposite a graveyard?
When they're not dead.

What was written on the hypochondriac's tombstone?
"I told you I was ill."

What did the father ghost say to the baby ghost?
"Fasten your sheet belt."

Where do undertakers go in October?
The Hearse of the Year Show.

Why are cemeteries in the middle of towns?
Because they're dead centres.

What do young ghosts write their homework in?
Exorcise books.

What keeps ghouls cheerful?
The knowledge that every shroud has a silver lining.

How did the ghost song-and-dance act make a living?
By appearing in television spooktaculars.

How did the glamorous ghoul earn her living?
She was a cover ghoul.

What kind of jewels do ghosts wear?
Tombstones.

What do you call a ghost's mother and father?
Transparents.

What are little ghosts dressed in when it rains?
Boo-ts and ghoul-oshes.

Why are ghosts bad at telling lies?
Because you can see right through them.

Who writes ghosts' jokes?
Crypt writers.

Where do mummies go if they want to swim?
The Dead Sea.

What kind of street does a ghost like best?
A dead end.

What do ghosts dance to?
Soul music.

What's the definition of a skeleton?
Bones with the person scraped off.

When do ghosts play tricks on each other?
On April Ghoul's Day.

What happened when the ghosts went on strike?
A skeleton staff took over.

What do ghosts say when a girl footballer is sent off?
Ban-she, ban-she!

What happened when a ghost asked for a brandy at his local pub?
The landlord said, "Sorry, we don't serve spirits."

How do ghosts learn songs?
They read the sheet music.

Where do ghosts go on holiday?
The Ghosta Brava.

Doctor, doctor, I keep thinking I'm an invisible ghost.
Did someone say something?

What do ghosts see at the theatre?
A phantomime.

Why did the ghost go to the funfair?
He wanted to go on the rollerghoster.

This woman wanted to marry a ghost.
I can't think what possessed her.

What did the ghost teacher say to her class?
"Watch the board and I'll go through it again."

What is a ghost-proof bicycle?
One with no spooks in it.

Where do ghosts live?
In dread-sitters.

Woman in bed: Aaagh! Aaagh! A ghost just floated into my room!
Ghost: Don't worry, madam, I'm just passing through.

What do ghosts write with?
Phantom pens.

What do you get if you cross a ghost with a packet of potato chips?
Snacks that go crunch in the night.

What do ghosts like in their coffee?
Evaporated milk.

How do you know you are haunted by a parrot?
He keeps saying, "Oooo's a pretty boy then?"

What happened to the poverty-stricken ghost?
He was dread-bare.

What is the ghosts' favourite quiz game?
Oooooo do you do.

Where do ghosts go for their holidays?
The Dead Sea.

What did the stupid ghost do?
He used to climb over walls.

What do ghosts eat?
Dread and butter pudding.

Which ghost sailed the seven seas looking for rubbish and blubber?
The ghost of BinBag the Whaler.

Why are ghosts at their loudest in August?
Because they're on their howlidays.

What's a ghost's favourite day of the week?
The one before Saturday, because it's Frightday.

What happened to the ghostly fishmonger?
He sold his sole to the devil.

Who is the most powerful ghoul?
Judge Dread.

Why did the ghost work at Scotland Yard?
He was the Chief In-Spectre.

What do you call the ghost who is a child-rearing expert?
Dr Spook.

What kind of ghoul has the best hearing?
The eeriest.

What is the ghosts' favourite song?
"Ooooo's that knocking at my door?"

Why don't you get locks on cemetery gates?
There's no point - all the ghosts have skeleton keys.

Who speaks at the ghosts' press conference?
The spooksperson.

Where do ghosts get an education?
High s-ghoul.

What do ghosts eat for dinner?
Ghoulash.

What do you call a prehistoric ghost?
A terror-dactyl.

What do ghouls eat for breakfast?
Dreaded wheat.

Which ghost ate too much porridge?
Ghouldilocks.

What's the most important member in the ghosts'
soccer team?
The Ghoulie.

What ghost is handy in the kitchen?
A recipe spook.

How does a ghost start a letter?
"Tomb it may concern."

Why were the ghosts wet and tired?
They had just dread-ged the lake.

How do ghouls like their
eggs cooked?
Terrifried.

Which airline do ghouls fly with?
British Scareways.

What do ghosts wear on wet days?
Khaghouls.

# Chapter Five

Does she have something on her mind?
Only if she's wearing a hat.

Laura: Whenever I go to the corner shop, the shopkeeper shakes my hand.
Lionel: I expect it's to make sure you don't put it in his till.

Passenger: Will this bus take me into town?
Driver: Which part?
Passenger: All of me, of course!

Joanne: How many people work in your college?
Johan: About half of them.

Father: Alan! You mustn't fight! You must learn to give and take!
Alan: But I did! I gave him a black eye and took his football!

Andrew: I'm too tired to mow the lawn.
Father: Listen, son, hard work never killed anyone.
Andrew: And I don't want to be the first!

Jane: Do you like me?
Wayne: As girls go, you're fine. And the sooner you go the better!

Harry: Every time I walk past a girl she sighs.
William: Yes _ with relief!

Michael: It's hard for my sister to eat.
Maureen: Why?
Michael: She can't bear to stop talking.

Boss: Are you willing to do an honest day's work?
Secretary: Yes, as long as you give me an honest week's pay for it.

Gordon: My wallet's full of big bills.
Graham: All unpaid, I expect.

When my dad finally passed his fourth-form spelling test he was so excited he cut himself shaving.

Fenton: You'll just have to give me credit.
Benton: Well, I'm certainly not giving you cash!

Peter: My brother wants to work badly.
Anita: As I remember, he usually does.

Dylan: I take lots of exercise.
Duncan: I thought so. That's why you're so long-winded.

Bernie: Why have you given me this piece of rope?
Ernie: They say if you give someone enough rope they'll hang themselves!

"Did you say he had a big mouth?"
"Put it this way, he's the only person I know who can eat a banana sideways!"

Your sister's boyfriend certainly has staying power. In fact, he never leaves.

My dad once stopped a man ill-treating a donkey. It was a case of brotherly love.

My brother's looking for a wife. Trouble is, he can't find a woman who loves him as much as he loves himself.

Son: How old are you, Dad?
Dad: Oh, around 35.
Son: I expect you've been around it a few times!

Son: Dad kept asking for glasses of water when he was in hospital.
Daughter: I expect that's how they knew he was going out of his mind.

They say he works eight hours and sleeps eight hours. Problem is, they're the same eight hours.

Jimmy: Is that lemonade OK?
Timmy: Yes. Why do you ask?
Jimmy: I just wondered if it was as sour as your face.

Jane: I'll cook dinner.
What would you like?
Shane: Good life
insurance.

Lee: Our family's
descended from royalty.
Dee: King Kong?

Jan: My little brother is a real pain.
Nan: Things could be worse.
Jan: How?
Nan: He could be twins.

"Do you like my new
baby sister? The
stork brought her."
"Hmm, it looks as if
the stork dropped
her on her head."

"My sister went on a crash diet."
"Is that why she looks a wreck?"

Cheryl: They say I have an infectious laugh.
Meryl: In that case don't laugh near me!

"He has a heart of gold."
"And teeth to match."

Penny: No one could call your dad a quitter.
Kenny: No, he's been sacked from every job he's ever had.

Mary: Do you think my sister's pretty?
Gary: Well, let's just say if you pulled her pigtail she'd probably say "oink, oink!"

"My brother's on a seafood diet."
"Really?"
"Yes, the more he sees food the more he eats."

"Does your brother keep himself clean?"
"Oh, yes. He takes a bath every month whether he needs one or not."

"His left eye must be fascinating."
"Why do you say that?"
"Because his right eye looks at it all the time."

Terry: When my mother was young she had a coming-out party.
Gerry: When they saw her they probably sent her back in again.

"I hear she was a war baby."
"I'm not surprised _ I expect her parents took one look at her and started fighting."

"My mother gets migraines."
"Probably because her halo's too tight."

"My boyfriend only has two faults _ everything he says and everything he does!"

"He thinks everyone worships the ground he crawled out of."

"I hear she doesn't care for a man's company."
"Not unless he owns it."

"They say he's a very careful person."
"Well, he likes to economize on soap and water."

"How can she be so fat? She eats like a bird!"
"Yes, a vulture!"

"She's so ugly that when a wasp stings her it shuts its eyes."

"They say he has a leaning towards blondes."
"Yes, but they keep pushing him back."

"Bill and Gill make a perfect pair, don't they?"
"They certainly do. She's a pill and he's a headache."

"Doesn't he look distinguished?"
"He'd look better if he were extinguished."

"He will never be a leader of men."
"No, but he's a great follower of women!"

"I hear he has a quick mind."
"Yes, he's a real scheme engine."

"That girl looks like Helen Black."
"She looks even worse in white."

Rich lady: That painting you did of me doesn't do me justice.
Artist: Madam, it's not justice you want, it's mercy!

Ronnie: I can trace my family tree way back.
Bonnie: Yes, back to the time you lived in it!

"A friend in need is _ someone to avoid!"

"They say her tongue's so sharp she can slice bread with it."

Laurie: We should all do our bit to clean up the environment.
Mother: I agree. You could start with your room.

The best way of saving money is to forget who you borrowed it from.

Owen: Thank you so much for lending me that money.
I shall be everlastingly in your debt.
Lenny: That's what I'm afraid of!

What's another name for pollution?
The effluence of affluence.

"Did you say he told good gags?"
"No, I said he needed one!"

"When it comes to helping others, she'll stop at nothing!"

"They say cleanliness is next to godliness."
"With some people it's next to impossible!"

"Does he tell lies?"
"Let's just say his memory exaggerates."

"Does he have big ears?"
"Let's just say he's very good at swatting flies."

"They say he's going places."
"The sooner the better!"

"Harry's very good for other people's health.
Whenever they see him coming they go for a long
walk!"

"I hear she's highly strung."
"She should be!"

"She's got so fat she can sit around a table all by
herself."

"I always think twice
before speaking."
"I expect it gives you
time to think up
something really nasty."

"He's a light eater."
"Yes, as soon as it's
light he starts eating!"

"She has real polish."
"Only on her shoes."

"She has an answer to every problem."
"Yes, but they're always wrong."

"He's watching his weight."
"Yes, watching it go up!"

# Chapter Six

AND FINALLY...
THE SWEETIE FACTORY

A girl in a sweetshop is one and a half metres tall and wears size four shoes. What does she weigh? Sweets.

A witch went into a sweet shop to buy some sweets. The man behind the counter said, "Gosh you are really ugly aren't you? I've never seen anyone as offensively hideous as you."
"Young man," she replied, "I didn't come in here to be insulted."
"Really," he said, "where do you usually go?"

What did the little demon do when he bought a house?
He called it Gnome Sweet Gnome.

Dear Sir, Knowing you do not eat sweets, I am
sending candy to your wife - and nuts to you.

Girl: My teacher's a peach.
Mother: You mean she's sweet.
Girl: No, she has a heart of stone.

Norbert: You remind me of a pie.
Noreen: Really? Am I sweet?
Norbert: No, but you've got some crust.

Samantha: Do you really love me?
Simon: Oh yes.
Samantha: Then whisper something soft and sweet in my ear.
Simon: Lemon meringue pie.

What is red, sweet and bites people in the neck?
A jampire.

What vegetable has the sweetest rhythm?
Sugar beet.

What is a toad's favourite sweet?
Lollihops.

What's sweet, sour, dangerous and travels?
Takeaway Kung food.

What's the difference between a huge, ugly, smelly monster and a sweet?
People like sweets.

What's the difference between a schoolteacher and a train?
One says spit out that sweet, the other says, choo, choo!

What's yellow and sweet and holds baby monkeys?
An Ape-ricot.

Why did Clarence sprinkle sugar all over his pillow?
He wanted to have sweet dreams.

Darren, who was rather fond of Sharon, gave her a
box of chocolates at break time on her birthday.
"Here you are," he said, blushing, "sweets to the
sweet."
"Oh, thanks," said Sharon. "Have a nut."

What favourite chocolate treat is found on the
seabed?
An oyster egg.

What is a French cat's favourite pudding?
Chocolate mousse.

Johnny collected lots of money from trick or treating and he went to the sweet shop to buy some chocolate.
"You should give that money to charity," said the shopkeeper.
Johnny thought for a moment and said, "No, I'll buy the chocolate. You give the money to charity."

Mum: Sue, there were two chocolate cakes in the larder yesterday, and now there's only one. Why?
Sue: I don't know. It must have been so dark I didn't see the other one.

What do you call a girl who's covered in chocolate?
Candy.

A monster walked into a hamburger restaurant and ordered a cheeseburger, fries and a chocolate milkshake. When he finished his meal he left £10 to pay the bill. The waiter, thinking that the monster probably wasn't very good at adding up, gave him only 50 pence change. At that moment another customer came in.
"Gosh, I've never seen a monster in here before," he said.
"And you won't be seeing me again," said the monster furiously, "not at those prices."

Waiter, waiter, what's this cockroach doing on my ice-cream sundae?
I think it's skiing downhill.

They answered a knock on the door and found a total stranger standing on the doorstep. "Excuse me for disturbing you, madam," he said politely, "but I pass your house every morning on my way to work, and I've noticed that every day you appear to be hitting your son on the head with a loaf of bread."
"That's right."
"Every day you hit him on the head with a loaf of bread, and yet this morning you were clouting him with a chocolate cake . . .?"
"Well, today is his birthday."

"Just think - a big chocolate ice cream, a bag of scrumptious toffees, and a seat at the cinema for ten pence."
"Did you get all that for ten pence?"
"No - but just think . . .!"

A family of tortoises went into a café for some ice cream. They sat down and were about to start when Father Tortoise said, "I think it's going to rain, Junior, will you pop home and fetch my umbrella?" So off went Junior for Father's umbrella, but three days later he still hadn't returned.
"I think, dear," said Mother Tortoise to Father Tortoise, "that we had better eat Junior's ice cream before it melts."
And a voice from the door said, "If you do that I won't go."

"I went to see my doctor to see if he could help me give up smoking."
"What did he say?"
"He suggested that every time I felt like a smoke I should reach for a bar of chocolate."
"Did that do any good?"
"No - I can't get the chocolate to light."

Why did Dracula go to the dentist?
He had fang decay.
Why did he have fang decay?
He was always eating fangcy cakes.

Girl: Did you like that cake Mrs Jones?
Mrs Jones: Yes, very much.
Girl: That's funny. My mum said you didn't have any taste.

Teacher: Who can tell me the difference between like and love?
Carol: I can, Miss. I like my mum and dad, but I love chocolate toffees.

Teacher: Order, children, order!
Daft Derek: Two chocolate ice creams and three orange lollipops, please.

What did the children do when
there were rock cakes for
lunch?
Took their pick.

Which flavour ice cream is Dracula's favourite?
Vein-illa.

How do you make a ghoul float?
Two scoops of ice cream, a bottle of coke and a slice
of ghoul.

What takes a lot of licks from a teacher without
complaint?
An ice cream.

One very hot day an extremely small man went into a café, put his newspaper on a table and went to the counter. But on returning with a cup of tea he saw that his place had been taken by a huge, bearded, ferocious-looking man of some 300 pounds in weight, and six feet nine inches in height.

"Excuse me," said the little man to the big man, "but you're sitting in my seat."

"Oh yeah?" snarled the big man. "Prove it!"

"Certainly. You're sitting on my ice cream."

Why is history like a fruit cake?
Because it's full of dates.

Witch: I'm looking for something to make my rock cakes light.
Shopkeeper: Sorry madam, we don't sell gas here.

What do witches eat at Halloween?
Spook-etti, Halloweenies, Devil's food cake and Boo-berry pie.

A woman woke her husband in the middle of the night. "There's a burglar downstairs eating the cake that I made this morning."
"Who shall I call," her husband said, "police or ambulance?"

"Mum, can I have two pieces of cake, please?"
"Certainly - take this piece and cut it in two!"

What cake wanted to rule the world?
Attila the Bun.

We had sponge cake for tea yesterday. Mum sponged
the flour from the woman next door . . . the milk
from our landlady . . . and ten pence for the gas
from the Avon lady.

My auntie Maud had so many candles on her last
birthday cake that all her party guests got sunburnt.

Auntie Nora: Have a piece of my Christmas cake,
dear. It's a new recipe.
Jenny: It's not very good, is it?
Auntie Nora: You have no taste, dear. The recipe
book says quite clearly that it's delicious.

The cookery teacher was in a delicatessen buying nuts for the afternoon's cake baking. "What kind of nuts would you like?" asked the shop assistant.

"Cashew," replied the teacher.

"Bless you," said the shop assistant. "What kind of nuts would you like?"

Witch: Try some of my sponge cake.

Wizard: It's a bit tough.

Witch: That's strange. I only bought the sponge from the chemist this morning.

Did you hear about the time Eddy's sister tried to make a birthday cake?

The candles melted in the oven.

What's the fastest cake in the world?

Meriiiiiiiiiiiiingue.

What swings from cake to cake
and tastes of almonds?
Tarzipan.

Countess Dracula: Say something soft and sweet
to me.
Dracula: Marshmallows, chocolate fudge cake . . .

Mother: I told you not to eat cake before supper.
Daughter: But Mum, it's part of my homework. "If
you take an eighth of a cake from a whole cake, how
much is left?"

I eat my peas with honey,
I've done it all my life.
It makes the peas taste funny,
but it keeps them on the knife!

A little boy went into a baker's. "How much are those cakes?" he asked.
"Two for 25 pence," said the baker.
"How much does one cost?" asked the boy.
"13 pence," said the baker.
"Then I'll take the other one for 12 pence!" said the boy.

Cookery mistress: Helen, what are the best things to put in a fruit cake?
Helen: Teeth!

"It's a pity you've gone on hunger strike," said the convict's wife on visiting day.
"Why?"
"I've put a file in your cake."

Young Jimmy was having tea with his Gran. "Would you like a biscuit?" she asked.
"Yes, please," replied Jimmy.
"What good manners you have," said his Gran. "I do like to hear young people say 'please' and 'thank you'."
"I'll say them both if I can have a big slice of that cake," replied Jimmy.

Where do bees keep
their money?
In a honey-box.

Why did the bees go on strike?
Because they wanted more honey and shorter working flowers.

What's red and wobbles on top of sponge cake and custard in the middle of Paris?
The Trifle Tower.

FROM A NEWSPAPER: Pieces of the giant cake were delivered to 200 senior citizens living locally in Mr Jones's van.

What's the worst kind of cake to have?
A stomach-ache.

What do you get if you cross a tin of baked beans with a birthday cake? A cake that blows out its own candles.

What kind of cake would most schoolchildren not mind going without?
A cake of soap.

How can you make cakes light?
Make them with petrol and decorate them with matches.

Why did daft Derek mop up his milk with his cake?
It was a sponge cake.

Teacher: Please don't eat off your knife, Betty, use a fork.
Betty: But, Miss, my fork leaks.

What did the bee say to the flower?
"Hello honey."

If bees make honey what do wasps make?
Waspberry jam.

What did the bee say to the wasp who he tried to
make honey?
Don't wasp your time!

What did a mummy's embalmer say when he was asked
how he kept the body so young?
"Tell them about the honey, mummy."

What do you get if you cross a flea with a rabbit?
A bug's bunny.

What's yellow, strong and very expensive?
A bunch of bionic bananas.

First man: I've just been stung by a bee.
Seconand man: How was that?
First man: I was charged £50 for a pot of honey.

Paddy was telling Mick of his plans to make a lot of money. "I intend to buy a dozen swarms of bees and every morning at dawn I'm going to let them into the park opposite my house to spend all the day making honey, while I relax."
"But the park doesn't open until nine o'clock," protested Mick.
"I realize that," said Paddy, "but I know where there's a hole in the fence."

What's the difference between an elephant and a biscuit?
You can dip your biscuit in your tea.


What did the biscuits say to the walnuts?
"You're nuts and we're crackers!"


Why was the biscuit unhappy?
Because its mother had been a wafer so long.


How do you get six monsters in a biscuit tin?
Take the biscuits out first.

What did the spider say to the bee?
"Your honey or your life."

Why do bees have sticky hair?
Because of the honey combs.

How did the baker get an electric shock?
He stood on a bun and a current ran up his leg.

"Those currant buns you sold me yesterday had three cockroaches in them," a woman complained over the phone to a baker.
"Sorry about that," said the baker. "If you bring the cockroaches back I'll give you the three currants I owe you."

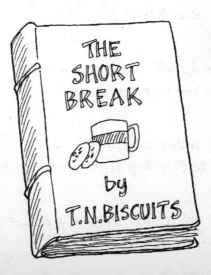

What did the middle-aged lady say as she tucked into her cream buns?

"I'm afraid all this food is going to waist."

Teacher: If I bought twenty-five buns for £1 what would each one be?

Riley: Stale, Miss.

Jerry: You remind me of a biscuit.

Terry: A lovely chocolate one?

Jerry: No, a gingernut because you're red-haired and stupid.

Why are bullies like bananas?
Because they're yellow and hang around in bunches.

Why is a crazy marmalade cat like a biscuit?
They're both ginger nuts.

Boy: What's black, slimy, with hairy legs and eyes on stalks?
Mum: Eat the biscuits and don't worry what's in the tin.

An irate woman burst into the baker's shop and said, "I sent my son in for two pounds of biscuits this morning but when I weighed them there was only one pound. I suggest you check your scales."
The baker looked at her calmly for a moment or two and then replied, "Madam, I suggest you weight your son."

"Jimmy, how many more times must I tell you to come away from that biscuit barrel?"
"No more, mum. It's empty."

"Don't eat the biscuits so fast - they'll keep."
"I know, but I want to eat as many as I can before I lose my appetite."

What did the biscuit say when its friend crossed the road?
Oh, crumbs!

There was a young man from Nepal
Who went to a fancy dress ball
He thought he would risk it
And go as a biscuit
But the dog ate him up in the hall.